GILGAMESH

A Verse Play

§

Wesleyan Poetry

Dedications & Other Darkhorses (1977)

Lost in the Bonewheel Factory (1979)

Copacetic (1984)

I Apologize for the Eyes in My Head (1986)

Toys in a Field (1986)

Dien Cai Dau (1988)

February in Sydney (1989)

Magic City (1992)

Neon Vernacular (1993)

Thieves of Paradise (1998)

Talking Dirty to the Gods (2000)

Pleasure Dome: New and Collected Poems (2001)

Taboo (2004)

Becoming a Successful Actor (2002)

Dramaturgy by Chad Gracia

The Death of Griffin Hunter (1998, Kirk Wood Bromley)

Washington: The American Revolution (1999, Kirk Wood Bromley)

Midnight Brainwash Revival (2000, Kirk Wood Bromley)

GILGAMESH

A Verse Play

Poetry by

Yusef Komunyakaa

Concept and dramaturgy by

Chad Gracia

WESLEYAN UNIVERSITY PRESS

MIDDLETOWN, CONNECTICUT

Published by Wesleyan University Press, Middletown, CT 06459

www.wesleyan.edu/wespress

ISBN 0-8195-6824-4 Cloth

Library of Congress Cataloging-in-Publication Data

Komunyakaa, Yusef.
    Gilgamesh : a verse play / poetry by Yusef Komunyakaa ; concept
and dramaturgy by Chad Gracia.
    p. cm. — (Wesleyan poetry)
    ISBN-13: 978-0-8195-6824-3 (alk. paper)
    ISBN-10: 0-8195-6824-4 (alk. paper)
    1. Gilgamesh—Adaptations. 2. Erech (Extinct city)—Kings and
rulers—Poetry. 3. Erech (Extinct city)—Kings and rulers—Drama.
4. Epic poetry, Assyro-Babylonian—Adaptations. 5. Epic poetry,
American.   I. Gracia, Chad. II. Gilgamesh. III. Title. IV. Series.
PS3561.O455G56 2006
813'.54—dc22   2006014045

Cover art taken from *The Revenge of Ishtar* © 1993 by Ludmila Zeman, published in
Canada by Tundra Books, Toronto, and in the United States by Tundra Books of North-
ern New York.

Contents

Collaborating with Komunyakaa:
The Creation of Gilgamesh[1]

By Chad Gracia

I first encountered the *Epic of Gilgamesh* twenty years ago, in Will Durant's grand tour of the ancient world, *Our Oriental Heritage*. I was amazed to discover that Gilgamesh, hero of the eponymous Sumerian epic, was a historical figure who ruled in Uruk (just south of modern-day Baghdad) around 2,600 B.C. A story cycle recounting his exploits coalesced in the following millennium, and Babylonian scribes codified the epic we now possess between 1,700 and 1,500 B.C. I hunted down a good translation and for weeks after reading it was haunted by the horrifying realization at the heart of the tale:

> Over his friend, Enkidu, Gilgamesh wept bitterly.
> He wandered through the wilderness and cried:
> "How can I rest? Despair is in my heart.
> I too shall die, for am I not like Enkidu?"[2]

About the same time, I was reading *The Denial of Death*, Ernest Becker's Pulitzer Prize-winning illumination of human nature, which argues that both personality and culture are deeply informed by an unconscious terror of mortality. What struck me was how similar these themes were to those that pervaded *Gilgamesh*. The passage of 46 centuries had not altered the basic

1. First published in Callaloo, Volume 28, Number 3. Reprinted with permission.
2. From Tablet IX, adapted from various sources by the author.

human dilemma: how to reconcile our seemingly infinite and soaring spirits with our finite and decaying bodies.

In fact, the epic insistently strikes at the problem of mortality and links Gilgamesh's fear of death with his inability to rule well, his mourning over his friend's corpse with his own unconscious fears, and his ultimate acceptance of his fate with a consolatory wisdom that echoes the great psychological and religious traditions of the world. Thus, in one of humankind's earliest stories, the essential questions are thoroughly explored. And they are explored with such beauty and power that the tale is rightly considered a masterpiece of literature.

§

I began to think about bringing the epic to the stage. Working for nearly a decade as a dramaturge (an editor and "story consultant" for playwrights) gave me experience nurturing scripts, while running a theater company gave me the opportunity to bring these scripts to the stage. I kept my eye open for a playwright who could bring Gilgamesh to life and do justice to the epic.

I first met Yusef Komunyakaa at a reading that I had helped produce of Glyn Maxwell's play *The Forever Waltz*. I was impressed with Yusef's quiet presence and struck by his mischievous smile. A few weeks later, we met again to discuss remounting *Shangri-la*, an operatic piece he had created with the composer Susie Ibarra. Yusef had penned several "poems for the stage" and was clearly interested in writing for the theater. I began to read his work more closely.

Among the many gems I discovered was "Ode to the Maggot," which hails the creature as a "little master of Earth," and reminds us that "no one gets to heaven / without going through you first." I immediately recalled the moment when Gilgamesh's comrade Enkidu dies, and the hero refuses to leave the side of his corpse for days. He drags himself away only after "a maggot crawled from Enkidu's nose." This description had always startled me. Rather than allow us the luxury of a perfumed and ritualized death scene, the poet chose to make the horror of Enkidu's decay and Gilgamesh's loss explicit and visceral. The maggot is a central and recurring character in both the epic and Yusef's work.

In fact, the more I read of Komunyakaa's poetry, the more convinced I became that he was perfectly suited to write *Gilgamesh*. The epic is about loss and death, and Yusef's work is infused with deep longing and a sharp awareness of mortality. I wanted the play to evoke the grit of a warrior-king's life. Yusef's poems of war in *Dien Cai Dau* were perfectly balanced between lyricism and realism, and depicted the horror of the soldier's life while at the same time infusing it with a metaphysical majesty.

So I faxed Yusef an outline of my ideas for an adaptation and a proposal for collaboration. Within a few weeks we were hammering out the basic structure of the play over coffee. Our strengths turned out to be complementary and our visions for the piece closely aligned. I know the stage; Yusef knows the word. I have a feel for character development; Yusef has a sophisticated sense of dramatic language. And we both respected the epic, but were not afraid to reimagine it when necessary.

Every other Sunday we'd meet with our cast—whom I chose not only for their acting ability, but also for their skill at analyzing text and their ear for story. After reading the week's scenes several times, I'd propose questions, probe to ensure that a plot point was clear, and try to envision how a moment would thrive—or wither—on stage. Yusef generally listened intently and spoke little. At times, he'd explain why he wrote what he did. He often ended debate with a simple pronouncement: "This is how it is."

After the reading, I'd uncork some wine and we'd venture into a more freewheeling and wide-ranging dialogue of the play's structure, characters, and emerging themes. Yusef joined enthusiastically in these discussions, which were as likely to focus on the nature of friendship or the pitfalls of romantic love as on the religious rituals of ancient Sumeria.

The day after each meeting, I sent Yusef a heavily notated script with summaries of the various problems we had identified. I would suggest cuts or additions and often reorder phrases to emphasize or clarify a point. Yusef digested these notes, adopted some and discarded others, and continued his work. A few days later we would talk through the evolving scene, and by the next reading most of our concerns had been addressed. At times, Yusef's transformation of a stumbling block into a dramatic coup was stunning—as in his creation of the wine merchant's wife, Geshtinanna, to clarify an aspect of Gilgamesh's personality.

Once the characters and structure were in place, we bade farewell to the actors and discussed the play line by line for several months. We cut mercilessly and polished incessantly. I stood on the lookout for remaining potholes and scouted opportunities for weaving disparate sections of the text together with imagery or metaphor. Often, if a line sounded off, I would simply point it out to Yusef and he'd speak several variants aloud, his eyes half shut and his head still. He'd roll the words around on his tongue and listen to how they harmonized. When he hit upon the right arrangement, he'd announce with a triumphant sparkle in his eyes: "That's it, isn't it?"

And so, twelve months after first meeting, our *Gilgamesh* was complete.

§

The Epic of Gilgamesh is one of humanity's most extraordinary stories. It provides a glimpse into the minds of those who lived nearly 5,000 years ago, at the cusp of history. In its depiction of riddling scorpions, gem gardens, and immortal sages, we find ourselves in a decidedly otherworldly realm. At the same time, it is precocious and provides an incisive portrayal of the human predicament that haunts us to this day. In our dramatic adaptation of *Gilgamesh*, we have attempted to capture both faces of the epic.

If we have succeeded, it is due largely to the genius of Yusef Komunyakaa. His voice and vision gave the work its magisterial tone, compelling drama, and rich poetry. Among the many instances of providence surrounding this project—which has been the most effortless and fruitful of my career—was the early realization that Yusef had a *Gilgamesh* waiting inside of him all along. My role was chiefly to assist at its birth, and I consider myself particularly lucky to have been a partner in this labor.

Acknowledgments

Special thanks to the artists who took part in workshops essential to creating *Gilgamesh*: Billy Atwell (music), Ronald Auguste, Alan Benditt, Bill Coelius, Megan Dullaghan, Canan Erguder, Dan Ilian, Billie James, Ruth Kulerman, Robert Laine, Sarah K. Lippmann, Leroy Logan, Julie Lund, Matthew Maher, Jim Milton (director), Matt Oberg, Franklin Ojeda Smith, Timothy Reynolds, Anne Richardson, Michael Ruby, Joshua Spafford, Emily Sweeney-Samuelson, and Tony Torn. Also to Richard Ryan and Paul Craig for their astute observations and input.

GILGAMESH

Prelude

A speechless world. The sound of running water and singing birds.
Music. Enkidu—a wild man dressed in leaves—romps with the
animals. A hunter's snare is center stage. A serpent basks in yel-
lowish light. A teenage boy, the Hunter's Son, stumbles upon this
moment of Eden.

An animal enters the hunter's snare. Commotion. Frenzy. Enkidu
releases the animal from the trap. The lights fade. The boy backs
away. The sound of fleeing footsteps.

Act I

Scene 1

Outside Uruk. The Hunter is center stage, sharpening the tip of a javelin.
His son runs in, almost breathless.

THE HUNTER'S SON

Father, I saw him!

THE HUNTER

Again?

THE HUNTER'S SON

I saw him dancing.
Dancing with the animals.

THE HUNTER

And?

THE HUNTER'S SON

He opened the snares
and freed our catch.

THE HUNTER

Did I not put my head
with a god's for days,
asking why is there blood
and hair in the snares
and not even a ghost of prey
left behind?
Now, I learn
a man-beast has broken
our oldest law!

THE HUNTER'S SON

He was so close,
I could almost touch him.

5

THE HUNTER

Would you grab a lion
or a bright-colored viper?

THE HUNTER'S SON

Father, I believe
he is almost a man.

THE HUNTER

Three weeks with no meat for our king.
There will be no mercy.

I will see if the beast can outrun my javelin.

THE HUNTER'S SON

Father, please do not kill him.
There are no words in his mouth,
but he wears a garment of leaves.
He is no beast.

THE HUNTER

What kind of man is he then?
We are here to see
into the past and the future,
and not to run amuck
with the dumb brutes of the forest
and rejoice in their darkness.

THE HUNTER'S SON

He had laughter in his eyes.

THE HUNTER

He has broken one
of our oldest laws.

THE HUNTER'S SON

But Father, to kill him
is to break an even older law.

Take my javelin
and go to the king in Uruk.
Tell him what you have seen,
and promise him our tribute
once he has driven off
or given us word
to kill this man-beast.
The Hunter and his son exit.

Scene 2

The citadel in Uruk. Gilgamesh sleeps and his mother, the goddess Nin-sun, enters.

NINSUN

Gilgamesh. Gilgamesh.

GILGAMESH

Mother?

NINSUN

Son, in your sleep last night
you were restless as a fretted lyre,
like a feverish child
wrestling a demon.

GILGAMESH

I glimpsed a star
falling from the sky,
and all the people of Uruk
crowded around the descending orb
aglow, and I was enraged and envious
and attempted to grab it up
in my arms, but my knees buckled
because I was too weak.

I was dying in my dream.
Mother, what does it mean?
I have never dreamt
such a dream before.

Just as you descended
from the heavens, this star
is a brother—a rival—a burden
you will try to lift,
but your knees will give
till you are kneeling on the ground
and gazing up at the sky.

GILGAMESH

I was dying.
The lights fade. The voices of the Chorus are heard.

CHORUS ONE

So, you wish
to see Gilgamesh?

CHORUS TWO

So, you wish
to see Gilgamesh?

CHORUS THREE

Well,
I shall tell you this
about our king Gilgamesh.
He is strong—

CHORUS ONE

He is strong
because he is part god.

CHORUS TWO

He is weak—

He is weak
because he is part man.

Stronger than
a human being—

But not a good king.

So, you wish
to see Gilgamesh?

So—

*The Chorus hears Gilgamesh's approach; they exit. Gilgamesh and the
Hunter's Son enter from opposite sides of the stage. The Hunter's Son falls
to his knees, facing Gilgamesh.*

GILGAMESH

Speak!
Are you here to steal
your king's ironclad time?

THE HUNTER'S SON

Sir—my father—my father—
my father is a great hunter.

GILGAMESH

There are a thousand
great hunters in Uruk.
And, so is your king
also a fierce hunter.

Why are you here
stealing my time,

and where is your tribute?

The Hunter's Son gains his composure. Gilgamesh gestures for him to rise.

THE HUNTER'S SON

My father is a great hunter, sir.
But a wild man has been robbing
our snares.

GILGAMESH

I always hear
the wildest litanies
on the day of credits
and debits.

THE HUNTER'S SON

He is almost a man.
I saw him dancing with the animals.

GILGAMESH

This tale is conjured to swindle me
of my rightful gifts of fur and meat.
I should cut your tongue out for such lies.

THE HUNTER'S SON

I ran the whole night,
the high trails
and the low trails
to get here, sir.

GILGAMESH

You have wasted footsteps.
To the armed guard.
Cut off a toe each day
and send it to his father.

THE HUNTER'S SON

Sir, please—

He opened the snares
and freed our catch.
I have spied on him—

He broke our oldest law.

GILGAMESH

He opened the snares
and freed a god-given catch?

THE HUNTER'S SON

My king, he is almost a man.
I saw him dancing with the animals.
Gilgamesh gestures to a guard and whispers into his ear.

GILGAMESH

We will see if this creature be man or beast.
To the armed guard.
Go to the temple and find the Woman of Red Sashes.
Bid her to use her charms
against the wild man
who frolics with the dumb brutes.
To the Hunter's Son.
If he succumbs to her, he is a man,
and you may live.

THE HUNTER'S SON

Please do not kill him.
He dances with the animals.
He is almost a man.
The Guard drags the Hunter's Son away. Another guard appears.

GUARD

Sir, the wine-maker's wife
kneels at the king's door.

GILGAMESH

Bid her enter.

The guard exits; Geshtinanna enters and kneels.

GILGAMESH

Rise.
What song is on your lips
this beautiful afternoon?

GESHTINANNA

Sir, I—

GILGAMESH

What is your name?

GESHTINANNA

Geshtinanna, sir.

GILGAMESH

I remember your face,
but I do not know from where.
Geshtinanna kneels again.

GESHTINANNA

May you pardon my tongue
and not apply the lash, my lord.

I come to the king's door
for my husband's sake, my lord.

GILGAMESH

Yes, you were a wild one
on your bridal night, Geshtinanna.

GESHTINANNA

My lord, I come to the king's door
for my husband's sake.

Seven days ago, your guards
broke down our door and dragged him off.

GILGAMESH

Your husband failed to honor
his tally of the sweetest
jugs of wine in Uruk.

GESHTINANNA

Now that my husband is in the stockade,
our house does not have bread
for the mouth of our son.

GILGAMESH

Do you not know
at least one beggar's chant?
Geshtinanna begins to disrobe.

GESHTINANNA

Do you remember these breasts?
Gilgamesh turns his back to her.

GILGAMESH

They are still succulent
as the ripest fruit,
but they are no longer
a virgin's breasts.

GESHTINANNA

Do you remember
the cries and promises
that leapt out of your mouth
that burning night?
Silence. Geshtinanna pulls her garment close. Gilgamesh faces her.

GILGAMESH

I am a king.
I honor the gods,
and you are blessed
that I honored my birthright.

Then honor my son with pity.
He may well be
your own flesh and blood!
Gilgamesh puts his hand over her mouth. The lights fade as he speaks.

I have no sons.
No daughter.
You cannot birth a king's child,
especially a king
who has the blood of gods
running through his veins.
You may have delicious lips,
a beautiful face,
but your body cannot hold
or vessel a king's blood.

And your husband
will stay his stay,
and pay Uruk his debt.
*Gilgamesh and Geshtinanna stand motionless in the semi-darkness. The
Chorus moves to the foreground.*

And we sing to you
all the old begats
up the Tigris and Euphrates.

And, yes, we know
all the old begats
from scripture and lore.

And a river god
fashioned woman from a man's rib

long before Marduk,
the Young Bull of the Sun
appeared on the horizon.

CHORUS TWO

And at the foot
of the ziggurat of Uruk
sat Gilgamesh as his mother
the divine Ninsun
told him how he was forged
from godhead and man.

CHORUS ONE

And etched on the rocks
is the Great Flood's blue-
black watermark.

CHORUS THREE

And on the cuneiforms
are written hundreds of begats
alongside the rising
and setting of Ishtar.

CHORUS ONE

But thousands of begats
are only written on air,
and they remain unnamed,
born forgotten,
or wrongly remembered.
The stage goes black.

Scene 3

A forest. The Woman of Red Sashes dances, holding a dagger. Her garment is translucent, revealing. She beckons Enkidu to her, but he hesitates. Finally, he reaches for her hair, touches her face, her breasts. Her sighs of pleasure draw him to her, closer and closer. Twilight.

THE WOMAN OF RED SASHES

Do you own a name?

Was your name
lost and betrayed
the same as mine,
and now you cannot remember
if you ever had a name?

A name would cast you away,
from the other animals,
from the wolves and jackals,
from the lions and deer,
from the rat and serpent.
Enkidu touches her thighs. She drops the dagger to the ground. The lights fade.
You are –
you are a meteor.
A smoldering star.
I call you Enkidu.
You are a man.
They fall to the ground. They couple. The sounds of love-making. Orgasm. Silence.
Enkidu is asleep. The Woman of Red Sashes is humming as she shaves him with her dagger. The silent animals are gazing at them. She oils his skin. She raises the dagger as if to kill him. She kisses Enkidu. He wakes to her kiss.

THE WOMAN OF RED SASHES

You were sleeping like a dead man.

ENKIDU

I am –
They are both surprised he has spoken.
I am,

THE WOMAN OF RED SASHES

I am a woman.

ENKIDU

I am – a man.
They laugh.
You are a woman.

THE WOMAN OF RED SASHES

God is language,
and all the ohs and ahs
weave man to woman.
They kiss. The sound of Humbaba's great sigh is heard but he is not seen.
The Woman of Red Sashes is startled. The animals recede.

THE WOMAN OF RED SASHES

What was that,
Enkidu?

ENKIDU

Humbaba.

THE WOMAN OF RED SASHES

Are we that close
to the Forbidden Forest?

I can smell Humbaba's cedars.
She grabs Enkidu's hand and they exit.

Scene 4

The Forbidden Forest. Humbaba sighs. The Goddess Ishtar enters.

ISHTAR

Did you call me,
Humbaba?

HUMBABA

Because I smell Enkidu's desire
in the air, his desire for a name,
you heard me say your name,
you heard me say Ishtar?

It was only a sigh of discord.
It was only a sigh of disgust.

ISHTAR

Oh slave and henchman
of the gods, how many years
have you lurked here
in this forest? Too many?

HUMBABA

Daughter of the moon,
mistress of the night,
great harlot,
save this venom
for your next lover.

ISHTAR

Humbaba.

HUMBABA

Will you devour me,
like the others?
Or will you simply
turn away when I call,
leaving me to die alone?

ISHTAR

Enough. You are vexed.

HUMBABA

I have been blessed and cursed
to know the future, and I know
Enkidu will come to me.

ISHTAR

He wouldn't dare.
The gods have sent him
to humble Gilgamesh, nothing more.

HUMBABA

He will seek out Gilgamesh.
The one you desire,
the name you call in your sleep.

ISHTAR

He is only part god.

HUMBABA

It is the part *man*
you desire, Ishtar.

ISHTAR

He is only a thought.

HUMBABA

I wonder
if the gods love me.

ISHTAR

The gods love you.
They have given you
the cedar forest,
the power of prophecy and revenge.

HUMBABA

The gods love their cedars.
They love the smell
of the rare wood.

They are possessed by great vanities.

I am blessed and cursed
to know half of the truth,
to know Enkidu
is on his way here.
But I do not know why.

ISHTAR

He is but a beast.

HUMBABA

But he dreams of being a man,
and dreams can make lunatics
out of men.
The lights fade.

Scene 5

Outside Uruk. A Traveler speaks to Enkidu and the Woman of Red Sashes.

THE TRAVELER

Are you like me,
merely passing through?

ENKIDU

Animals come down from the hills.

THE TRAVELER

The shepherd told me about you,
how this woman from the city
brought you out of nowhere
up to his front door.

THE WOMAN OF RED SASHES

Did I bring Enkidu here,

or was he sleepwalking
and I followed him here?

THE TRAVELER

You do not tell the truth.

THE WOMAN OF RED SASHES

If we told you the truth
you would not believe us.

THE TRAVELER

If *you* told me the truth.

The shepherd says that you guard
his flock, that the predators
seem to know you, to know –
even the lion and the jackal
now keep away from his fenceline.

ENKIDU

I can only do what I was born
to do, my friend.

THE TRAVELER

The shepherd says it seems as if
your presence keeps them away.

THE WOMAN OF RED SASHES

The animals love him.

THE TRAVELER

Does love keep them
at bay?

THE WOMAN OF RED SASHES

Their love is so simple.

THE TRAVELER

They can love you

one moment,
and tear you apart
the next moment.

ENKIDU

It is hard to be
an animal.

THE TRAVELER

It is harder to be
a man.
Enkidu takes the Woman of Red Sashes' hand.

ENKIDU

One morning I began
walking with the sun at my back,
as if I had walked that trail before
in an animal's hide or another heart,
and you followed me, led me away
from my friends in the forest.

THE WOMAN OF RED SASHES

I did not lead you away
from your friends,
but I did let my heart
guide me here.

THE TRAVELER

The shepherd worships you.
How does it feel to be
a man's protector,
without any bloody fear
of claw and fang?

ENKIDU

I do not know.
I can only do
what I was born to do.

THE TRAVELER

Then you are a godsend,
if ever a godsend was
goodness.

ENKIDU

Goodness?

THE TRAVELER

I know goodness
when I see goodness.

THE WOMAN OF RED SASHES

How do you measure
a man's
or a woman's
goodness?

THE TRAVELER

I measure a man's goodness
by thinking of Gilgamesh.

ENKIDU

Who is this Gilgamesh?

THE TRAVELER

Gilgamesh is our king.
He was born part god,
and we were born to pay
tribute.

ENKIDU

But if one has only a dream
in his head, can a king
also take away this?

THE TRAVELER

Even dreams are not safe.
In Uruk, I found a virgin

sworn to be my bride,
awaiting my touch.
But I know Gilgamesh
will be the first to knock
upon the chamber door.

THE WOMAN OF RED SASHES

A king is always first
to ease his thirst.

ENKIDU

Have you also pleased his thirst?

THE WOMAN OF RED SASHES

Gilgamesh is my king.

ENKIDU

He is not a good king!
I shall go to Uruk
and tell him so!

You will guide me to Uruk
so I can tell him so.

THE WOMAN OF RED SASHES

He will kill you
with his bare hands.

ENKIDU

He is not a good king,
and I shall tell him so.

THE WOMAN OF RED SASHES

Gilgamesh is part god.
*Enkidu speaks as he exits, with the Woman of Red Sashes following
him.*

ENKIDU

I am a man.

What is a god?
What is a god
without man?
The lights begin to fade.

He will kill you
with his bare hands.
The stage goes dark.

Scene 6

The citadel in Uruk. Gilgamesh has just awakened. Ninsun gives him a steamy cup of brew.

You were tossing and turning
in your sleep again,
Son.

In my dream,
I tried to lift an ax
but the people crowded around
and my knees buckled
as if I were an old man.
My spirit left me
and my god-given strength
was sapped.

I ache from pate to toes,
as if I have wrestled with myself
in the dirt the whole night.

Mother, why am I suffering man's hurt?
If I have god in me
my knees should never buckle.

The ax is a man.
A tool. A weapon.
A friend. It depends
on where the two of you
stand in the sunlight,
how the sun strikes the blade.
The tiredness woven into your muscles,
it will all lift away
as this friend grows near.
He is the other half
of your true heart.

GILGAMESH

I hope your words are true,
because I glimpse rage
in the eyes of my people,
and it weighs like a brick
in my belly.
Gilgamesh begins to dress.

NINSUN

I am afraid
I have fed you
too much food of the gods –
words, myths, and delicacies
bitter and sweet.
I am afraid
the part of you
that is a god
has eaten the heart of the man.
Ninsun exits. The lights fade.

Scene 7

Uruk. The roar of a crowd. The beating of drums. The wail of a ram's horn. Enkidu, the Woman of Red Sashes and the Traveler enter. The Chorus enters opposite them.

CHORUS ONE

He looks like Gilgamesh.

CHORUS TWO

He is a bit shorter—

CHORUS THREE

But you can see
he is very strong.

CHORUS ONE

Man-beast of the Steppe,
we heard you were on your way here.

CHORUS TWO

He looks like Gilgamesh—

CHORUS THREE

And his feet seem rooted
to the good earth.

Enkidu positions himself in a doorway, his arms akimbo. Gilgamesh enters. He pushes the Woman of Red Sashes aside. A fury is on Enkidu's face. Gilgamesh walks up to the doorway; Enkidu is a bulwark of presence and confidence. He blocks Gilgamesh's entrance.

GILGAMESH

Step aside of the threshold
and bow down.
Do you—
do you know who I am?

I am Gilgamesh, a king.

ENKIDU

I am Enkidu.

GILGAMESH

If you do not bow
and step aside,
nothing but worms will live
in your skull by moonrise!
Gilgamesh attempts to shove past.

ENKIDU

Because you are a king,
Do you think—

CHORUS ONE

Gilgamesh—

GILGAMESH

Step aside! Bow to your king,
and step aside!

CHORUS ONE & TWO

Enkidu—

GILGAMESH

I am here to honor
my god-given birthright.

ENKIDU

Is every virgin
yours to deflower?

CHORUS THREE

Gilgamesh—

GILGAMESH

Am I not the King of Uruk?

CHORUS ONE, TWO, & THREE

Enkidu—

Somebody pray for them!

ENKIDU

One man does not birth
another man.

GILGAMESH

I have killed men
twice your size.
Are you a fool?

ENKIDU

I lived in the forest
and ran with the lion
and the wolf,
and I fear you.

GILGAMESH

On your knees, you—
The Traveler exits.

CHORUS ONE

Gilgamesh—

CHORUS ONE & TWO

Enkidu—

GILGAMESH

I am almost a god.

CHORUS THREE

Gilgamesh—

CHORUS ONE, TWO, & THREE

Enkidu—

ENKIDU

How can you
be almost a god

and not yet a man?

                              GILGAMESH

You are more animal
than man—

                         CHORUS ONE

Where are the gods?

                              GILGAMESH

But I shall still
make you bow down
like any other subject
under the blue skies of Uruk.

                              ENKIDU

I am not bowing.
I am not running.

                         CHORUS TWO

Two bulls locking horns.

                              ENKIDU

I stand here.
I stand here.

                              GILGAMESH

You stand here.
I am giving you a chance
to back down, to act—

                         CHORUS ONE

Where are the gods?

                              ENKIDU

I stand here
stock still.

                              GILGAMESH

Bow down

and say you never
touched your king.

ENKIDU

You are not a good king.

GILGAMESH

Treason.

CHORUS ONE

They are about to kill each other!

CHORUS TWO

There is blood in the moon!

CHORUS ONE

Where are the gods?
They fight, struggling in the embrace of each other's strength, till they
are eye to eye, straining against one another. Gilgamesh's knees buckle;
Enkidu is exhausted.

GILGAMESH

Are you that falling star?
If so, I have been waiting
for you.

ENKIDU

I am Enkidu.
They stand back, eyeing each other.

GILGAMESH

Toehold to toehold,
eyeball to eyeball,
measure to measure, I believe
you are the one I have been searching for.

ENKIDU

I am Enkidu.

GILGAMESH

You have the skull of a jackal.
I have dreamt of you.

ENKIDU

And you have the heart of a bull.
Have I also dreamt of you?
Gilgamesh claps his hands and an attendant approaches.

GILGAMESH

Wine!
Why are you here?

ENKIDU

To battle this man
who masquerades as a god.

GILGAMESH

You masquerade
as an animal.

ENKIDU

I am a man.
Silence. The Woman of Red Sashes moves away. A servant brings wine.

GILGAMESH

Well, let us be ourselves.
And let us drink.

ENKIDU

You are still bloated
by pleasure and greed.

GILGAMESH

You are foolhardy.
You are the man
I want by my side.
*They drink. A great rumble is heard as the city gates close in the distance.
A spotlight comes up on the Woman of Red Sashes kneeling before an
altar. She shakes a gourd rattle. Incense burns.*

Oh, Ninsun,
Wild Cow of the Enclosure,
Great Queen
who stands between man and god,
mother to our dread king,
did I not call your name
before I journeyed into the forest
as the king's emissary?

I have again ushered a dream
of flesh into flesh, and left
two men facing each other
like an open wound,
like two brutish brothers
kneeling at their mother's feet.

How many times must I be
summoned from this temple,
pressed into the service of men,
before I am allowed to be
merely a woman?

I hurt to be lost again
in the forbidden mountains
and valleys of my own dreams,
to stand at the unholy brink.

I hurt to be called by a name,
to be a mother,
to sleep in my own bed,
and to bake loaves of bread.

*The spotlight fades on the Woman of Red Sashes; Gilgamesh and Enkidu
are still drinking wine and talking.*

GILGAMESH

As if spoken from a daydream.
There is a cedar forest
clouds dip down to touch,
to linger on like a great question.
They are the gold of the gods
guarded by a brute force,
and I have dreamt of them
since I was a boy.
I would crawl to the forest edge,
to the edge of one thousand years
of silence, clutching my little war ax
and whisper Humbaba-Humbaba-Humbaba
under my breath until I could feel
my muscles growing stronger.

Friend, if you were at my side,
measuring footstep for footstep,
the tallest of those cedars
would fall and rise as a gate
to our city, and no squad
of renegades or clan's battering ram
could smash it to a heap of splinters.

ENKIDU

Your name is feared in a dozen tongues,
and you do not need a stronger gate
to protect this city.

GILGAMESH

I know greed
can make lunatics out of men,
and Uruk needs a taller gate
between them and their dreams.

ENKIDU

But you are part god.

GILGAMESH

And you have slept with animals
beside a creek.
Gilgamesh claps his hands, and a guard appears.
Bring me the strongest bow
and my quiver of arrows.
And two double-edged swords
to light our path with blood.
Gilgamesh waves the guard away. He speaks to Enkidu.
We will face Humbaba
and cut down his forest.

ENKIDU

You say I am foolhardy,
but you are more foolhardy.

When I slept beside the animals
and drank from the same spring
as they, we knew
to never venture among those trees.

GILGAMESH

You cowered before,
but you did not know Gilgamesh.
With Humbaba's cedars
we will build a gate that summons us to glory.
The dream I have in my head
will bring us luck.
We will strip his evil
down to death sighs among the leaves.

ENKIDU

Why encourage his anger
and wrath?

35

Because he is evil.
And, together, we are
stronger then he is.

ENKIDU

But when I think of Humbaba
the strength drains out of my arms,
and I feel like a returning warrior
standing before a locked door
with two empty sleeves.
Gilgamesh and Enkidu embrace. The lights fade.

Scene 8

Uruk. The Council of Elders is meeting. Each wears a distinctive mask.

ELDER ONE

What were Gilgamesh's words,
what did he say, how did he say it?
He said this: *my* dream has begun to come true
because *I* have a brother, a friend
who has sworn to go with *me*
into battle against evil,
against Humbaba.

I. Me. It is not our battle,
but we will be drummed into it.

ELDER TWO

He did come to us, for our blessing,
and this alone seems like a different
Gilgamesh. Just two days ago—we—
this council of elders was speaking of Humbaba
as if we had vinegar in our mouths.
When the king spoke to us

36

it was like hearing our words
come back at us.

Gilgamesh is right: It is a pity
the daring passed down through legend,
from dust to flesh—our old audacity
has drained out of us. Now,
the young men seem without courage.
They are like fat, yellow pods
the worms have eaten empty.

ELDER ONE
But is our Gilgamesh
an heir to bravery?
Has not the rallying cry
laid dead on his tongue
for years, while he rattled
the doors of the bridal chambers?
Is this not his legacy?

ELDER TWO
We crave someone to bless the coffins
and fill the coffers of our city.
Maybe this is the path to tomorrow,
to have Humbaba do the job
each of us is too weak to do.

ELDER THREE
It seems the gods have been busy
plotting against our king.

ELDER TWO
Or, maybe they have been busy
plotting against us.
Gilgamesh enters; the Elders rise and file past him, each nodding an
affirmative.

GILGAMESH

The Old Ones have nodded Yes,
saying Yes to my request
to cut down Humbaba.

Scene 9

Gilgamesh's chambers. He is half-dressed, in deep thought. An attendant stands at his side, holding a garment. Ninsun is outside the door.

NINSUN

Step aside you brute,
you yesman to the King.
Ninsun appears in the doorway, the guard tugging at her sleeve. Gilgamesh waves him away.

GILGAMESH

Mother, you cannot
charge into my chambers.

NINSUN

If you were a good king—

GILGAMESH

I am a good king.

NINSUN

You are not even a good son.

GILGAMESH

I am.

NINSUN

Do you know
what brought me
through this door?
What I have been thinking
the whole day?

I have been thinking:
my son does not love me.

GILGAMESH

Of course, I love you.

NINSUN

I praised the god in you
night and day
since you took your first breath.

GILGAMESH

And that is why I love you.

NINSUN

Suppose I tell you
that you are less god
than I bragged into your head?

GILGAMESH

I would say,
my mother loves me
and she does not
want me to fight Humbaba.

But there is no turning back,
though I love you dearly.

NINSUN

Your father was a mortal
and he depended
on the goodness of the gods.

GILGAMESH

But your godhead lives
within me too, and will prevail.

39

NINSUN

I love your human weakness,
but I am afraid.

GILGAMESH

Of course.

NINSUN

Maybe you love
my gift for interpreting
the gods. I am good
for something, for some ends,
a reader of dreams.

GILGAMESH

I love your wisdom,
but also I love your face.
I love your dark eyes.
I love your smile
summer and winter mornings.

NINSUN

When is the last time
you gave your mother flowers?

GILGAMESH

A king does not pick flowers.

NINSUN

You used to venture
to the edge of the woods
and return with the most
wounded bouquets.

GILGAMESH

A king does not pick flowers,
especially a king who is part god.

NINSUN

You were this tall
She measures the air with her hands.
the last time you picked flowers
and gave me their brightness.

GILGAMESH

You know it is bad luck
to gaze upon a warrior
who is dressing for battle.
Gilgamesh retreats and is joined by Enkidu. They dress for battle. Nin-
sun lights incense.

NINSUN

Shamash, the dear god
I pray to night and day,
why have you given my son
a solid heart and restless feet
hinged between yes and no? And,
now, he is off to battle Humbaba,
to rid our world of evil.
Invincibility is the food of the gods,
the bittersweet delicacy,
and I fed him an ambrosial glut.
But is he only a man
sent to do a god's job?
Why did you
plant this damnable seed
in them, Shamash?
Wanderlust will swarm
his brain past
the very end.

He will suffer the downfall
of your scheme against evil.
Please protect him against

this spirituous dream.
Ninsun blows out the incense. She calls to Enkidu in a whisper.

Enkidu. Enkidu.

ENKIDU

Yes, Ninsun.

NINSUN

They say the people of Uruk
prayed to the gods for you,
that the gods shaped you
from a hunk of clay
and tossed you into the forest.

You are not my son,
but you are dear
as a son, Enkidu.

ENKIDU

Once, I was almost a man,
and now I am almost a son.

NINSUN

You are dear as Gilgamesh,
who is part my own flesh
and blood, and I beg you
to protect your spirit brother.

ENKIDU

We go as one
among Humbaba's cedars.
I do not wish to go
but we have been fitted
for battle.

NINSUN

When Gilgamesh

gets a thought in his head
it turns into mindless
flesh and blood.
Guard him against himself.
Ninsun places a charm around Enkidu's neck. The lights fade.

Scene 10

The Forbidden Forest. Shadows of trees reflect across the stage; sounds of birds and animals. Gilgamesh and Enkidu trek into the forest. The voices of the Chorus are heard.

CHORUS ONE

And our hearts followed
Gilgamesh and Enkidu—

CHORUS TWO

Over hills and down
into the valley—

CHORUS THREE

Up among the oldest trees.

CHORUS ONE

And our hearts followed them
for one day—

CHORUS TWO

Then two days—

CHORUS THREE

And then three days.

CHORUS ONE

And an echo of Ninsun's voice
bled across the sky.

NINSUN (OFFSTAGE)

"And I beg the gods

43

to keep a good eye
on Gilgamesh and Enkidu."

ENKIDU

In the forest
I learned to read
the minds of the animals,
their growls and songs.
And I learned that terror
lives among these cedars.

Now, I wonder: Does the thought of evil
beget evil, and can only evil kill evil?

GILGAMESH

Is the thought of Humbaba
sapping your strength?

ENKIDU

Again, for the last time
I say this again:
If one does not have a plot
he will come to know
it is not strength alone
that wins a battle.

GILGAMESH

I have this.
He cuts the air with his sword.
We have perfect swords.

ENKIDU

Do not wager your blade
and strength against Humbaba.
He is stronger than three oxen,
stronger than a dozen good men.

GILGAMESH

He is not swift
as my sword.

ENKIDU

Humbaba can wheel
and turn like a fire-chariot.
Like a great bird
in midair.

GILGAMESH

But still, he cannot think
fast as this sword.
I give you my word:
Humbaba will die
with my name in his mouth.

ENKIDU

Perhaps. Like the strongest
animals in the Steppe—
what I learned from them
in their endless tussle
against each other
is this—

GILGAMESH

Are we not here
to fight? Go on,
lay me up against
more and more sorrow.
Enkidu grabs Gilgamesh and holds him in place.

ENKIDU

Do not take another step
till we cast a plot.
The call of a single bird. Silence.

GILGAMESH

What did you learn
from the animals?

ENKIDU

I learned to look
prey dead in the eyes.
I learned a tough grace.

GILGAMESH

So, you did not learn
any ways of battle?

ENKIDU

Humbaba is a giant.
He is stronger
than a flank of soldiers.

GILGAMESH

But we are swifter than he is,
and if we can get close enough
we can make his strength
burn out in time.

ENKIDU

And then he will grow angry.

GILGAMESH

And we will let his anger
run amuck if we do not
slay him from the start.

ENKIDU

He can hear a worm
crawling at the forest edge,
and when he blinks
a sparrow eats the worm.

GILGAMESH

You make Humbaba into a god.

ENKIDU

He is death.

GILGAMESH

Then, at least,
our people will say,
we died in battle
against death.

ENKIDU

I shall take this path,
and you stand here.
If he calls your name,
do not answer. Wait
till he is almost on your sword.
*Gilgamesh nods and Enkidu exits. The call of a lone bird. Silence. The
marching-rolling sound of Humbaba's approach is heard—circular. He
is not seen. "Humbaba" grows into a resounding echo.*

HUMBABA

I am Humbaba.

GILGAMESH

Your name is
your death rattle.

HUMBABA

For ten days
I counted your footsteps,
and now here you stand
at the forbidden threshold.

GILGAMESH

If you can read minds,

then you know
what I am here to do.

So, Gilgamesh and Enkidu,
you wish to die
by calling my name?
How can you kill me
when you cannot even see me?
I can go inside your heart
and turn your knees to mud.
Gilgamesh falls to his knees.
I can make you bark
like a dog at his master's gate.
If you call me Evil,
I shall be more than Evil.
Ishtar enters.

ISHTAR

Please spare him, Humbaba.

HUMBABA

He who casts an eye on these trees
and a blind eye
upon our sacred laws,
be he king or swine-bastard,
part god or fool,
begs my vengeance.

ISHTAR

Brandish him till he
calls my name,
but please do not kill him.

HUMBABA

The gods have woven vengeance
out of my heart
and there is no mercy.

GILGAMESH

Your cedars are like towers
I dreamt of in another world,
and dead or alive
I shall scale them
as if the gods made them
while thinking of me.

And when I close my eyes
you do not exist.
Enkidu appears.

HUMBABA

Did you not know
this is the forbidden gate
where all human questions are answered,
and to fight me
it is like fighting yourself?
*Enkidu charges Humbaba, cutting off his huge arms. Humbaba's howl
is thunderous.*

ENKIDU

Look what you led me to do.
Look what fear made me do.

HUMBABA

Have mercy on me.

ENKIDU

We will let you live.
And may your wounds
eternally remind you
of the evil in your heart.

ISHTAR

No.

HUMBABA

I have no mother
or father. I am
the beginning and the end,
almost as if I never was.
The sound of great sobbing.

ENKIDU

Humbaba is no god.
He is a small beast
in a big forest.
He is only a roar
among the night trees.
*Gilgamesh swings his sword again and again, hewing Humbaba to
pieces.*

HUMBABA

Enkidu. Enkidu. Enkidu. Enkidu.
The lights fade.

Scene 11

*The Forbidden Forest. Humbaba's head half-fills the rear of the stage.
Gilgamesh and Enkidu have finished their bath, readying themselves for
the trip back to Uruk. Ishtar enters; she carries Gilgamesh's robe and
crown.*

ISHTAR

The gods are in an uproar
over your slaying of Humbaba,
and I see your crime
displayed like a trophy.

GILGAMESH

A man has to sometimes kill
so he may live.

ISHTAR

I am here to spare you.
I am the go-between.

GILGAMESH

What have I to fear?

ISHTAR

You are a fool.
Do you think
you are above death?

GILGAMESH

My mother has taught me well
the genus and hex of my name.

ISHTAR

You have slain the protector of the cedars,
and not even Enkidu can protect you
from my father's wrath.

GILGAMESH

Humbaba was marked to die.

ISHTAR

You have broken a sacred law.
Wed me and my father's wrath
will dwindle.

GILGAMESH

Ishtar, you know
you ask of me
what would grind my heart
to a fistful of dust.

You are an old harlot
whose heart belongs to no man.
You loved the lion

and dug a pit for him.
Your love is war.

We shall see
how many damnations
my father casts at your feet.

Ishtar runs off. The stage goes black; an uproar rattles the darkness. The Bull of Heaven descends and attacks Gilgamesh and Enkidu. After a great struggle, they kill the beast, then fall to the ground, exhausted. The sounds of sleep; night sounds of the forest; Ishtar tiptoes on stage and touches Enkidu with a long bone; she exits. Silence. They wake.

ENKIDU

I cannot sleep.
I cannot stop
dreaming two or three nightmares
in one.

GILGAMESH

I was sleeping like a dead man.

ENKIDU

Because we slew Humbaba
one of us must now die.

GILGAMESH

The gods will protect us.

ENKIDU

In my dream, the gods
singled me out to die.

GILGAMESH

I shall speak for you.
I shall fend for you.

I struck at Evil's first

52

and last birth-roots,
and we both are innocent.

ENKIDU

Can we be innocent
with blood on our hands?

GILGAMESH

Evil drew us to it.
When we locked hands
we were meant to destroy it.

ENKIDU

They have drawn my name
in the dirt and marked me down
for the underworld.
Enkidu is almost in tears.

GILGAMESH

The fever is ravaging you,
my brother. Do not bow.
We must return to Uruk,
and build our gate.

ENKIDU

May the termites grow
into a cloud
against Humbaba's forest.
May the Hunter
and the Woman of Red Sashes
who stole my soul
from the animals,
from my friends—
may those two
unbury the dead
in unending dreams.

What is this?
Enkidu?

Humbaba's forbidden forest
that guarded evil down to the last mite
and the first prayer,
I would now chop it down
to a hill of splinters
if I could raise my arm
to swing an ax.

We will stand together.

Shamash, old mantra
of godhead and earthworms,
I curse your heart
for bringing me to this
juncture, to this crook
in the long road home.

I am a king.
I have never led
an army to the brink,
and death has never looked me
in the eye.

Here you are, old friends
from the forest, from the Steppe,
you now linger again with me
beside this deep,
unlit door. This place that is

no place. This echo from the dark
where death and breath are the same
sound rolling down from the hills,
up to the edge of sky. Again,
I taste the she-wolf's milk,
and her howl is my cry
at the edge of these woods.
We are a drunken god's
feverish deed and prank.

Enkidu dies. Gilgamesh closes Enkidu's eyes and kisses him on the cheek.
He takes the charm from around his neck and tosses it on the ground. He
paces in a circle; exits, and returns, dragging a few branches of laurel. He
lets the branches fall to the ground and sits beside the corpse. Silence.

GILGAMESH

And I sit here—
And I sit here—
And I sit here
in my immense aloneness.
And I sit here—
And I sit here—
And I sit here
in my unbelievable grief.
And I sit here—
And I sit here—
And I sit here
in a great silence
older than this forest,
older than these hills,
older than this valley.
And I sit here—
And I sit here—
And I sit here
with the animals
on the edge of my grief,

55

their bright eyes
gazing at my heart.

And I sit here—
And I sit here—
And I sit here
till—
till one day
turns into three—
and I cannot stop
staring at Death
till a maggot
drops from Enkidu's
nose.

Gilgamesh rises and begins to cover the corpse with the branches. The lights fade.

End of Act I.

Act II

Scene 1

The Forbidden Forest. Enkidu has been uncovered, the laurel branches thrown aside. Gilgamesh is trying to wake him. He paces in a circle, his eyes downcast. He picks up the charm from the ground and ties it around his neck. He says "Enkidu" as he paces, and the name is woven through the Chorus.

CHORUS ONE

Grief is eating Gilgamesh—

CHORUS TWO

Down to a birthmark
on his right shoulderblade.

CHORUS THREE

The animals of the forest
are now mourning
a great unsayable loss.
Gilgamesh places the branches again on Enkidu.

GILGAMESH

My friend. My brother.
I shall go on a quest
to find that timeless man
who crossed the desert
and rounded the sea,
and I shall give you back
to life, breath and song,
to argument and laughter.

I shall find Utnapishtam.
Gilgamesh exits.

And Gilgamesh began to walk
toward the setting sun—

Into the day's last rays of light—

And soon he entered a ravenous
darkness.

And Gilgamesh walked
till it seemed he was walking
backwards—

Till he was lost
in his own mind, in his heart—

And for many days he thought
he would never see the sun
again—

Till the city of Uruk
was without walls—

Only the shadow-
faces of his people.

And then
Gilgamesh was standing there
gazing up at the mountains of Mashu.
The lights fade.

Scene 2

The Mountains of Mashu. Gilgamesh is face-to-face with Scorpion Man and Scorpion Woman, their stingers hanging menacingly over their heads. He averts his eyes.

SCORPION MAN

You are at the threshold.

GILGAMESH

Move aside.

SCORPION WOMAN

I can see into your heart.

SCORPION MAN

I can see into your soul.

GILGAMESH

Let me pass.

SCORPION MAN

Only gods dare
to travel this road.

GILGAMESH

You are looking at a god.
Now let me pass.

SCORPION MAN

Why is there so much woe
in your voice? Are you lost?

SCORPION WOMAN

He is not lost enough.

GILGAMESH

The love of a friend
is stealing my mind,
and I must speak
to the first man

who walked this path,
to Utnapishtam.

SCORPION WOMAN

Do you not know
this is the beginning
and the end?

SCORPION MAN

Look at us. Look into our eyes.

GILGAMESH

I know one glimpse into your eyes
means my last breath.

SCORPION WOMAN

Your mother was a god,
and you may look at me.

SCORPION MAN

You must face death every step
of the long, unmerciful way.
Gilgamesh looks into their eyes.

SCORPION WOMAN

You are not ready.
Turn around and go back
into the light.

SCORPION MAN

Beyond this road,
beyond these mountains,
there is only darkness.
Beyond here,
your bounty will only be grief.

GILGAMESH

This was my bounty before I came!
Grief?! The worms

of grief are already
inside my mind, my heart,
my blood, already inside
my spleen! Open the gate
so I may confront the father of Grief.

SCORPION MAN

The cold and heat
will make you kneel
in the red dust.

GILGAMESH

I know.
I know pain.
I know loss.
And I know ice,
snow, and heat.
I know darkness
and I know death.
Now, open the gate
to the mountains.

SCORPION MAN

As you wish!
The gate between
earth and hell
now stands agape!

SCORPION WOMAN

You must face death every step
of the long, unmerciful way.
The stage goes black.

Scene 3

Beyond the mountains. Gilgamesh speaks from the darkness, while sounds of owls and wolves emanate from all around, growing into an echo of laughter.

Where am I? Am I
in that place where light is
darkness, where happiness
always springs into fear,
where the young grow old
overnight, where immeasurable
death blooms in every seed
on the Road of the Sun?

This road is neither ahead
nor behind, and now the days
of darkness turn into blindness
and my eyes refuse to set
on any path, where ascension
is descension and descension
is a bottomless pit
in the sky. I hear nothing
but grief at my side: Enkidu
are you walking with me, am I
measuring my footprints in yours?
The lights ease up slowly.
This valley? Where am I?
This valley agleam with stones,
these fruit trees in bloom—
some flowering and others
hanging with their burden
of bright fruits. Am I in hell?
Do I hear the Bull of Heaven?
Gilgamesh falls to the earth. The lights fade.

Scene 4

The brink of the world. Siduri, a barmaid, is at work. Gilgamesh wears tattered animal skins—wild-looking in his disarray. The lights come up. Gilgamesh shields his eyes in the brightness; he stands before Siduri.

SIDURI

Who are you?

GILGAMESH

I am—
I am.

SIDURI

Are you a murderer
running away
from the laws of man
and the gods?

GILGAMESH

I am—
I am a king
Siduri laughs.

SIDURI

Who are you
when you are not
swollen with dreams?

GILGAMESH

I am a king.
I am Gilgamesh.

SIDURI

You are mad.
Gilgamesh is a king,
and you are clothed
in tattered skins.
Almost an animal.

63

GILGAMESH

I killed—

I killed—
I killed Humbaba.
Who are you?

SIDURI

If you are Gilgamesh,
the slayer of evil,
why is silence
in your eyes?

GILGAMESH

I have a friend
who fought shoulder
to shoulder with me,
from beginning to the end.

When he died,
I almost had to break my arms
to break my embrace.
I could not surrender
his friendship.

SIDURI

Why are you here?

GILGAMESH

I need—
I am—
I am lost.
Siduri begins to wipe the dirt from his face with the hem of her long garment.

SIDURI

Yes. Yes. Yes. Yes. Yes.
Siduri disrobes him, tossing aside the tattered animal skins. She fetches

a basin of water and oils, returning to Gilgamesh. Siduri uncorks an earthen jug of brew, handing it to Gilgamesh. They both periodically sip from the jug. She begins plucking a lyre-like instrument; she hands Gilgamesh a small drum, smiling. She sings.

When I laugh
my laughter
comes back to me
threefold
at the threshold,
like an echo of mystery
from across the sea.

When I laugh
my laughter
comes back to me
with a lover's
sweet perchance
and goat-footed romance
to make the soul dance
my laughter
comes back to me
like a bright bird
from across the sea.
Siduri and Gilgamesh dance.
When I laugh
my laughter
comes back to me
outside death's doorway
at the edge of this bay,
and I am almost happy
when my laughter
comes back to me.
Siduri and Gilgamesh fall to the ground. They kiss. They laugh. Gilgamesh half-rises, but Siduri forces him down. The lights fade slowly.

Show me again how
to touch a woman—
though the gods
may have sent you
to block my path.

I am Siduri.
I am only a barmaid
at the brink, between
worlds.

Siduri,
tutor me till
stars tremble in the water.

Tutor me till
a viper sheds the skin
of a demi-god—

the sash of a bright garment
in the morning light of dusk.

Tutor me till
I am born backwards in time,
and sorrow does not
know my name.

Teach me how to be a king.
Teach me how to die a man.
The lights fade. The sounds of love. The soft sounds of sleep. A cock crows.
The lights come up. Siduri and Gilgamesh lie in each other's arms. She
kisses him awake.

SIDURI

Today,
we must begin
like yesterday ended.

GILGAMESH

Where am I?
Where is Enkidu?
How long have I slept?

I was walking in the darkness
for days, many-many days,
and I stepped into a blinding light.

SIDURI

And love was staring
into your eyes.

GILGAMESH

And desire faced me
like hot winds
of another world.

SIDURI

I am of this world.
There is no other world.

GILGAMESH

What do you mean?
I have journeyed through
other worlds, but my journey
is not over. Even if I am
on the edge of forever.

SIDURI

Only death is forever,
unless you are a god.

But you kiss like a man,
and you sigh like a man.

There are children in me,
and we could cherish them
till we are back in that
other world. There are days
and nights, and there are suns
and moons.

GILGAMESH

Enkidu is dead.

SIDURI

But you are alive.
Your heart still beats.
Your eyes still see
and your fingers still touch.
Stay here. Across the river
there is only more death.

GILGAMESH

I have been through darkness
to arrive at the edge of this river.
And, I shall journey
through darkness again
and again, till I am at some way station
in the damnable fog
facing Utnapishtam.
Siduri attempts to kiss Gilgamesh; he pulls away.

SIDURI

I have danced
to keep you here.
I have given you
in the deep night
everything I can give

a god or a man,
and if you wish to journey on—

GILGAMESH

I have no choice—

SIDURI

I can only say, Go.
If you do not know
paradise, go.
Go. Run to the void
with your arms flung wide,
and die a human's everlasting
death. Go!

GILGAMESH

Point me the way.
Tell me the way
to Utnapishtam,
and I shall follow
this trail back here.

SIDURI

Is Utnapishtam a legend
or a part of this earth?

GILGAMESH

He is the only man
who fought the shadows
and won.
I have heard he lives
across the river.

SIDURI

Then you must find
Urshanabi, the young boatman.
Only he can lead you
across the river of death.

69

GILGAMESH

I only wish to hear of life.

SIDURI

There are stone sentinels
along the path, guarding him.

Since self-love blinds you,
I am fool enough to open my door
again if silence does not claim you
before this day ends.
Siduri points the direction.

GILGAMESH

Self-love does not
blind me, but loss
has almost torn my heart out.
Gilgamesh pulls the war ax from his belt; he charges off the stage.

SIDURI

Go!
Silence. Gilgamesh rushes back. They hug and kiss, and then stand gazing at each other. Siduri pulls away.

Go!
Gilgamesh exits. The lights fade.

Scene 5

Further along the riverbank. Gilgamesh is smashing the last of the stone sentinels with his ax. He sinks to the ground, exhausted.

GILGAMESH

Why did I smash these statues?
Why did I leave Siduri?
Where has Enkidu gone?
He hears nearby laughter.

70

Who are you?
More laughter. Silence
A spotlight comes up on an old man. He is dancing.

URSHANABI

I am the one you are speaking with.

GILGAMESH

I am Gilgamesh.
I have journeyed from Uruk.

URSHANABI

Look at you.
You have destroyed
the sacred sentinels,
as if you are the last
to follow his folly here.

GILGAMESH

I am in search of Urshanabi.

URSHANABI

Urshanabi?
Who could that be?

GILGAMESH

He is a young man
who dares to trouble
this water.

URSHANABI

I recall such a man,
but that was long ago.
I have not seen him here
in many-many years.
Gilgamesh sinks again to the ground.

GILGAMESH

He is the one man alive

who could ferry me
across to Utnapishtam.

You angered the gods
when you smashed the sacred stones
that brought you here.

GILGAMESH

I smashed the statues
so that no evil could track me.
Where is the young boatman?
I was told he would be here.

URSHANABI

Yes, you are a pale sack of bones.
Yes, your eyes pool with grief.
Yes, I am the young boatman.
And you seek Utnapishtam's herb.

GILGAMESH

You are old.

URSHANABI

I suppose that is true.
I suppose even here
the days and nights have passed.
Even here
decay rules the body.

GILGAMESH

My brother saved me
from Humbaba. I spoke,
and he began to dream
my dreams. My pain
became his.
He was my dearest friend,
and now I am his prisoner.

URSHANABI

You seek the herb
for yourself.

GILGAMESH

I seek life
for my friend.
For Enkidu.

URSHANABI

The heart is a selfish forest
of twisted vines.

GILGAMESH

Ferryman, will you guide
me to Utnapishtam?

URSHANABI

As you destroyed your friend,
as you destroyed the sacred sentinels,
you will destroy yourself
if you risk that journey.

GILGAMESH

That may be,
but I must speak
with the man who walked
this forsaken path before me.

URSHANABI

Believe me, what you seek
is not worth the price.
You cannot pluck
endless fruit
from the same vine.

GILGAMESH

If you refuse to guide me,
then I shall go alone.

URSHANABI

You will die.

GILGAMESH

I have looked death in the eye
and I have traveled a valley
where sprigs of life jut like light
out of stone.
I have tasted love at the brink.
I suppose I am ready for death.

URSHANABI

Take your ax
into the forest
and chop down five
long, straight branches
and set them in pitch,
and these poles
will help to ferry you
across death's great river.
Gilgamesh charges off stage; the sound of his ax is heard.

Most men turn around halfway.
This one is different.
But we shall see
if his heart is still strong
after the waters of death
have eaten away the first pole,
the second pole, the third pole,
and then the fourth pole.

Lost one driven by grief,
I shall help you
set the boat asway
on the troubled river,

but you must bear
the hard journey alone.

Will you cower down in the boat
and beg the gods to turn around?

I think so. Yes. Yes.
These lost men always turn around
three or four strokes away
from Utnapishtam's threshold.
They always turn back.
*The light fades. The sound of waves—water birds—wind. The shadow
of a boat. Gilgamesh's silhouette rocks back and forth. Lightning and
thunder. Semi-darkness.*

Scene 6

*Utnapishtam's island. Lights come up. Utnapishtam gazes down at Gil-
gamesh, who is sprawled nude on the ground, motionless.*

UTNAPISHTAM

Did the river give us
another dead man,
another lost soul?
Utnapishtam shakes his head. Urshanabi speaks from across the river.

URSHANABI

Old Seer,
I tried to warn him
but he was determined
to set eyes on you.

UTNAPISHTAM

And it looks as if
he has only set eyes
on the unknown.

URSHANABI

My eyes followed him
into the deep night,
and I knew he was mad
when I saw him dip the last pole
into the black water, and then,
to carry the pitiful boat on,
he stripped and turned
his rags into a sail.

UTNAPISHTAM

I see where the salty wind
began to eat him alive.

URSHANABI

I tried to tell him
the night winds are blades
whittling a bone,
but he would not stop
talking about his dead
brother—his friend—
someone called Enkidu.
Gilgamesh stirs; Utnapishtam kneels beside him.

GILGAMESH

Enkidu!

UTNAPISHTAM

The sound of a name
has awakened the dead.

GILGAMESH

I am Gilgamesh.
I am king of Uruk.

UTNAPISHTAM

Why would a king seek
a mad man's journey?

GILGAMESH

You are legendary.

UTNAPISHTAM

Legend, myth, lies, dreams,
beliefs, sometimes I do not know
one from the other.
Did lies bring you here?
Did dreams bring you here?

GILGAMESH

Hope brought me here.
Utnapishtam takes down the makeshift sail.

UTNAPISHTAM

Hope also brought me here.

Or, perhaps it was fear.
The fear of death.
The fear of life.
The fear of death in life.

GILGAMESH

The unknown
and the unknowable?
Utnapishtam hands Gilgamesh the tattered clothes.

UTNAPISHTAM

The gods told me what to do
and I did not second-guess them.
A voice leapt out of a whirlwind
and said, Citizen of Shurrupak,
you must build a vessel
and take two of every kind aboard.

Sometimes, I do not know
if I am blessed or cursed

by the arch-god Ea
who warned that Enlil
the war god desired me
barred from Shurrupak.

GILGAMESH
You followed your heart here.

UTNAPISHTAM
I followed
the echoes of rival gods.

GILGAMESH
At least
it was not divine deception.

UTNAPISHTAM
I followed
the echoes of their wounded
blessings. I called out
to the citizens of Shurrupak
in the lingering light of the Euphrates,
and I said: Come, please come,
and help me drag timbers from the forest,
help me peg and wedge them together
till there are seven stories,
and nine chambers in each story,
and we raised the ark
that had come to me
in a dream.

GILGAMESH
When a man turns
against his dream,
he turns against himself
and his manhood withers.

And, then, we snared
animals in the Steppe—
birds that lit the fields—
male and female.
We hustled them aboard.
Carpenters and masons
and bridge builders.

GILGAMESH

At least, there were others
wound up in your dream.
You were not absolutely alone.

UTNAPISHTAM

Word went out for a navigator,
and at the last moment
one stumbled in, just before
Ea ordered me to close the great
door. Lightning and thunder
rumbled in the day-lit sky,
and darkness roared over
the city of Shurrupak.

GILGAMESH

It is dangerous for us
when the gods are in an uproar.

UTNAPISHTAM

Lost children searched
for weeping mothers.

Men cursed the names
of their fathers
as the rain dug their graves.

Women disrobed.
Dogs bayed for their masters.
Doors of houses floated past.
Livestock tried to swim against
the wild current.

A few men leapt
from the trembling vessel,
but somehow I stood
stockstill.

GILGAMESH

Please do not say
you were not afraid.

UTNAPISHTAM

I was terrified.

GILGAMESH

Like a child
standing between the blows
of two grown-ups.

But you were not absolutely alone.

UTNAPISHTAM

Maybe I was alone
with faces around me.

GILGAMESH

Yes, maybe you are right.
I did have Enkidu with me
in my aloneness.
His ghost has tracked me here.

UTNAPISHTAM

We floated for many days
and nights, till the waters receded.

Maybe I was alone.

Maybe you were feeling
alone like a king.
The aloneness
of being told that you are special.

UTNAPISHTAM

Is that what made me scared?

Ea had singled me out,
and I had obeyed the echo,
and then Enlil the war god
was there like a silence before
a storm, blessing me and my family,
saying: Once you were a mere man,
but now you and your wife
are like gods. You
shall live an eternal life
beside the river of death.
The lights fade.

Scene 7

*Utnapishtam's island. A small room of a makeshift house. Gilgamesh
sleeps in a corner.*

UTNAPISHTAM'S WIFE

Did you talk this stranger to death?

UTNAPISHTAM

No.
The river almost took him.
Is it fortune or a curse
they come seeking?

UTNAPISHTAM'S WIFE

Are my old kisses
a fortune or a curse?

UTNAPISHTAM

I do not understand.

UTNAPISHTAM'S WIFE

I was wondering if the lost ones
are afraid of loneliness,
that they tire so easily
of routine, of the simple things.

UTNAPISHTAM

But this one
almost wore out his soul
to arrive here.

UTNAPISHTAM'S WIFE

Do you glimpse yourself
in him, Utnapishtam?

UTNAPISHTAM

He is still young and strong
enough to kill a bear.

UTNAPISHTAM'S WIFE

But he does not possess
the strength to endure
the shape of the eternal question.
What does he know about loneliness?

If we did not hear a harp
and flute in the unearthly silence,
immortality would be a curse.
If we could not decipher
ten thousand shades
in the moon's shadow

or in the call of a single sparrow,
the endless days and nights
would be a relentless curse.
Gilgamesh stirs; he opens his eyes.

UTNAPISHTAM

You have answered my question.

GILGAMESH

I also have a question.

UTNAPISHTAM'S WIFE

Yes. You are a question
in the heart of loneliness
that we see and live as grace.

GILGAMESH

My brother Enkidu died
to save me from Humbaba,
and legend brought me
to your threshold.

UTNAPISHTAM'S WIFE

You have come here
in the name of a friend,
and not your own fear?

GILGAMESH

Perhaps I came for Enkidu.
Perhaps I came here for Gilgamesh.

UTNAPISHTAM

Other men have worn out their hearts
to get here, with only their names
in their mouths.

UTNAPISHTAM'S WIFE

And perhaps that is why
they gave up a few strokes away

from our threshold.
Utnapishtam touches Gilgamesh's shoulder.

GILGAMESH

I journeyed here
for wisdom, to face
possibility.

UTNAPISHTAM

Your praise cuts into an old man's heart,
but I have nothing to give that can cure
each breath you take.
The two men cannot look at each other; they stare at the floor.

UTNAPISHTAM'S WIFE

He has journeyed so far.
Have you forgotten
how grief took hold
of your heart and wrestled you
to the ground? I remember
you begging for a word, a hint,
anything to break its grip.

GILGAMESH

I would like to see Enkidu.
I would like to live.
Utnapishtam gazes into Gilgamesh's eyes.

UTNAPISHTAM

Pain has also unfurled
her endless logbook
against me.
When I look into your eyes,
I know what I am seeing.

I will tell you a secret—
a secret my lips

84

have never revealed.
There is a thorny flower
that grows in the depths
of the river.
A plant
my wife calls Old-Man-
Becomes-Young-Man.
And it appears as if
it does not belong on earth.

UTNAPISHTAM'S WIFE

But it can give new life.
Gilgamesh hugs Utnapishtam and his wife. He rushes off stage. The
lights fade.

Scene 8

A riverside. Gilgamesh crawls in, water dripping from his body. He holds
a sprig of watercress between his teeth. He seems aglow. He unties the
stones laced around his feet. He places the sprig of watercress on the
ground beside him.

GILGAMESH

I dove down into the singing
water, down into the falling
silence, down into a breathless
season of foreverness. At first,
I cursed Utnapishtam's name.
When the last whisper of hope
drained out of me, I turned
and saw the thorny plant.
I almost drowned with laughter,
but I had not come so far
to be defeated.

And, oh, yes: there it was—

a sprig, a thorny flower,
aglow in the watery darkness.
I wanted to eat a leaf or two,
but I was afraid.
Gilgamesh picks up the plant and dances around.

GILGAMESH

I have it! Life. Life. Life. Life.
*A yellowish light flows over the stage. Gilgamesh is exhausted and he
falls asleep, the watercress beside him. Silence. Songbirds nearby. A ser-
pent crawls across the stage and stops before the plant. It snaps up the
sprig.*
*Gilgamesh leaps to his feet, his ax drawn. He screams and lets the ax
drop to the ground; he falls to his knees, weeping. The serpent sheds its
skin and crawls away. The lights fade.*

Scene 9

*Uruk. The beating of drums and the wailing of flutes. Gilgamesh en-
ters, carrying a large grass sack on his shoulders—Enkidu's remains. The
Chorus speaks.*

CHORUS ONE

He looks like the king.

CHORUS TWO

He looks like the king's ghost.

CHORUS THREE

If he is the king,
where is his friend—?

CHORUS ONE

His brother.

CHORUS TWO

Where is Enkidu?

Did the king kill his brother?

The king slew his brother.

The king killed Enkidu.

The king killed his friend.

The king has come back
from the dead.

We can smell the grave.

A field of jasmine
could not kill the stench.

He looks like a mad man
carrying death on his back.

*The armed guard and two Elders rush Gilgamesh off stage. Noise. An
uproar.*

The king has come back to life.

He crawled out of the grave
and is here to rule Uruk again.

Our king has come home.

He is carrying grief
in a grass sack.
The lights fade.

Scene 10

Uruk. Gilgamesh stands before the Council of Elders.

ELDER ONE

You are dead.

GILGAMESH

Do I look like a ghost
to you?

ELDER TWO

King, do I dare say this?

When you first entered the gate,
you looked like the great-
grandfather of a ghost.

GILGAMESH

I could not leave him
in the Forbidden Forest
for ravens to pick clean his bones,
for the rain's horrible work.

ELDER THREE

You brought back
a sack of bones,
but we will give Enkidu
a hero's ceremony of crossed swords
and a volley of drums.

ELDER TWO

He died protecting our king.

I could not acquiesce to the worms,
to the quiet tyranny of springtime.

ELDER THREE

When I saw you carrying your burden
as carrion birds circled overhead
patrolling the dusky sky,
I thought I was in purgatory.

GILGAMESH

That is what grief does
to a mortal being.
Keeper of the almshouse
or prideful king.

Take rations to the poor.
Send our royal doctors
to the sick.
Rally the holymen,
the prophets, and the soothsayers.
Open up the prisons.

ELDER ONE

King, sir,
please reign in yourself.
Gilgamesh claps his hands and an armed guard appears.

GILGAMESH

Release the hunter's son.
The guard exits. Gilgamesh speaks to the elders.

Make sure the boy
is paid a good year's wage
of gold from the royal purse.

And, prepare the biggest feast

the city of Uruk has ever known.
The lights fade.

Scene 11

*Gilgamesh's chambers. Music in the distance. Ninsun serves Gilgamesh
a mug of hot brew.*

NINSUN

To honor your death,
the elders sacrificed
seven rams, and a cloud
of incense rose around me
for seven days and seven nights.

GILGAMESH

But I am alive,
mother.

NINSUN

I had given you up
to the grave.

GILGAMESH

I have given up
half of myself
to the grave.
She hugs him.

NINSUN

I am happy
to see you.

But I am saddened
to see your spirit brother's face
only when I close my eyes.

GILGAMESH

I will rub Enkidu's ashes
on my face and into my hair,
but I will never forget him.

NINSUN

I made him promise
to block harm's path
for you, son.

GILGAMESH

He was a perfect friend.
A perfect brother.

NINSUN

You met grief on a winding path,
but did you also glimpse a bloom
you never before set eyes on?

GILGAMESH

In the dark, my eyes
lost their sharpness.

Till I set eyes on Siduri.

NINSUN

Siduri?

GILGAMESH

A beautiful mystery
at earth's end.

NINSUN

And it was hard for you
to continue your journey.

GILGAMESH

It was almost hard
as losing Enkidu,

but I did not know that
till I lost the thorny flower
and knew I would not return
to those watery depths.

NINSUN

Sometimes we learn the music
of our hearts too late.

GILGAMESH

But it would be worse
if we never learned it.
*The sound of drums and flutes; distant voices. Gilgamesh hands his
mother a flower. The spotlight fades on Ninsun and Gilgamesh.*

Scene 12

*Uruk. The Hunter enters, dressed in animal skins, holding a lance at
the ready. His Son runs on to the stage. They hug each other.*

THE HUNTER

What did the king
feed you?

THE HUNTER'S SON

He fed us bone gruel
of guinea fowl and bear,
of rabbit and quail.
He fed us bits of fat,
gristle, and gall.

THE HUNTER

I am not an assassin,
but my heart is swollen
with a father's righteousness.
The son places some gold coins in the father's hand.
And now he tries to buy his soul

back with some gold coins.
He is a beast.

THE HUNTER'S SON

Father, I believe he is a man.

THE HUNTER

Where is your anger?

THE HUNTER'S SON

Laughter from the high windows
always found me in my lowest hours,
and sometimes I did not know
any difference from the baying hounds.
The musicians enter.
I dreamt every night of the Steppe,
how big the sky is.
Gilgamesh enters, accompanied by the armed guard and Ninsun. Gilgamesh's face and hair are colored with ash. Voices fill the stage.

GILGAMESH

When I walked through the gates of Uruk,
I knew the old Gilgamesh had died.

Fear was in every bone of my body.
The Woman of Red Sashes enters.
But I knew I would not be alone.
*Gilgamesh walks over to the Woman of Red Sashes; he kisses her hand;
she bows.*

GILGAMESH

My dear Siduri.

THE WOMAN OF RED SASHES

I am not Siduri.
I am only a temple priestess,
without a name.

93

GILGAMESH

May I call you Siduri?

THE WOMAN OF RED SASHES

I am not Siduri.

But you may teach me
everything your eyes have seen
in the darkness.

GILGAMESH

No, teach me.

Teach me how to live
without a name.

Teach me how to be a king.
Teach me to die a man.
Music fills the stage.

The End

About the Authors

YUSEF KOMUNYAKAA is a professor in the Creative Writing Program at New York University. He has won the Pulitzer Prize for Poetry and been awarded the Ruth Lilly Poetry Prize.

CHAD GRACIA is the Development Director of the New Globe Theater and former Executive Director of Inverse Theater. He has edited six verse plays and is the creator of *ActorTips*, a weekly newsletter read by over 50,000 actors.